DOLPHINS SET I

WHITE-SIDED DOLPHINS

Megan M. Gunderson
ABDO Publishing Company

visit us at
www.abdopublishing.com

Published by ABDO Publishing Company, 8000 West 78th Street, Edina, Minnesota 55439. Copyright © 2011 by Abdo Consulting Group, Inc. International copyrights reserved in all countries. No part of this book may be reproduced in any form without written permission from the publisher. The Checkerboard Library™ is a trademark and logo of ABDO Publishing Company.

Printed in the United States of America, North Mankato, Minnesota.
042010
092010

 PRINTED ON RECYCLED PAPER

Cover Photo: Peter Arnold
Interior Photos: © Danny Frank / SeaPics.com p. 17; Fred Paquet-MICS Photo p. 21;
    Getty Images p. 8; © James D. Watt / SeaPics.com p. 19;
    © Lori Mazzuca / SeaPics.com p. 13; National Geographic Stock p. 15;
    Peter Arnold p. 5; Uko Gorter pp. 7, 9

Editor: Tamara L. Britton
Art Direction & Cover Design: Neil Klinepier

Library of Congress Cataloging-in-Publication Data

Gunderson, Megan M., 1981-
  White-sided dolphins / Megan M. Gunderson.
      p. cm. -- (Dolphins)
  Includes index.
  ISBN 978-1-61613-416-7
  1. Atlantic white-sided dolphin--Juvenile literature. I. Title.
  QL737.C432G86 2010
  599.53--dc22
                                    2010001579

CONTENTS

WHITE-SIDED DOLPHINS

White-sided dolphins live in northern ocean waters. They are **cetaceans** from the family **Delphinidae**. All cetaceans are mammals. So, white-sided dolphins are **warm-blooded** and nurse their young with milk. They must swim to the water's surface to breathe air.

Scientists recognize two different white-sided dolphin species. These are the Pacific white-sided dolphin and the Atlantic white-sided dolphin.

White-sided dolphins are closely related to white-beaked, hourglass, and Peale's dolphins. They all belong to the genus *Lagenorhynchus*. That name is long! So, members of this group are called lags for short.

Dolphins breathe through a single blowhole. This nostril is located on the top of the head.

SIZE, SHAPE, AND COLOR

Male white-sided dolphins grow longer and heavier than females. Atlantic white-sided dolphins average 6 to 9 feet (1.9 to 2.8 m) in length. They weigh 365 to 510 pounds (165 to 230 kg). Pacific white-sided dolphins grow 6 to 8 feet (1.7 to 2.5 m) long. They weigh 190 to 400 pounds (85 to 180 kg).

White-sided dolphins have robust bodies. The Atlantic white-sided dolphin has a short, thick beak. Its dorsal fin curves backward. The Pacific species hardly has a beak at all! Its dorsal fin is very large. With age, the fin may become curved like a hook.

The white-sided dolphin's back is dark gray. Its sides are lighter gray, and its belly is white. The

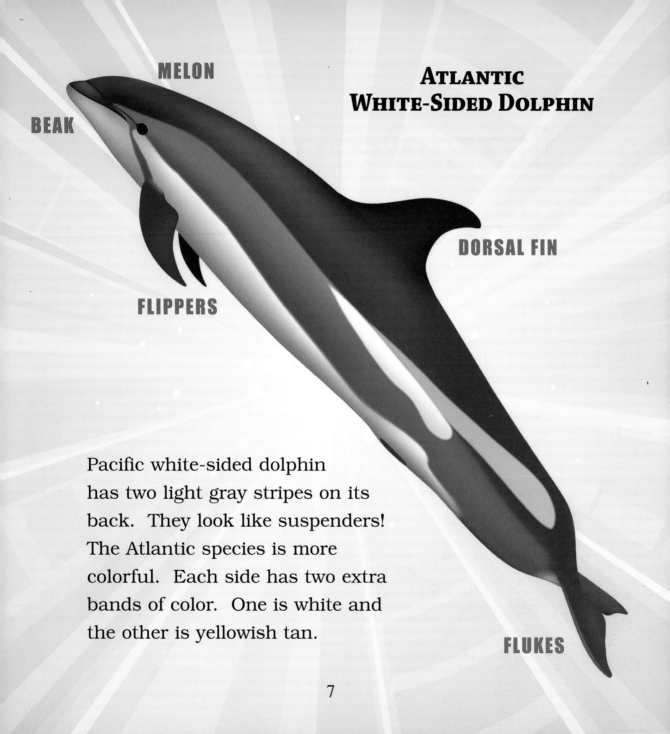

MELON

BEAK

ATLANTIC
WHITE-SIDED DOLPHIN

DORSAL FIN

FLIPPERS

Pacific white-sided dolphin
has two light gray stripes on its
back. They look like suspenders!
The Atlantic species is more
colorful. Each side has two extra
bands of color. One is white and
the other is yellowish tan.

FLUKES

WHERE THEY LIVE

Pacific white-sided dolphins will swim close to shore if water there is deep.

White-sided dolphins live in **temperate** and **subpolar** ocean waters. Their names reflect their ranges. Atlantic white-sided dolphins live in the North Atlantic Ocean. Pacific white-sided dolphins live in the North Pacific Ocean.

Atlantic white-sided dolphins **migrate** south in winter and north in summer. Some also move offshore in winter and inshore in summer. Atlantic

Where Do White-Sided Dolphins Live?

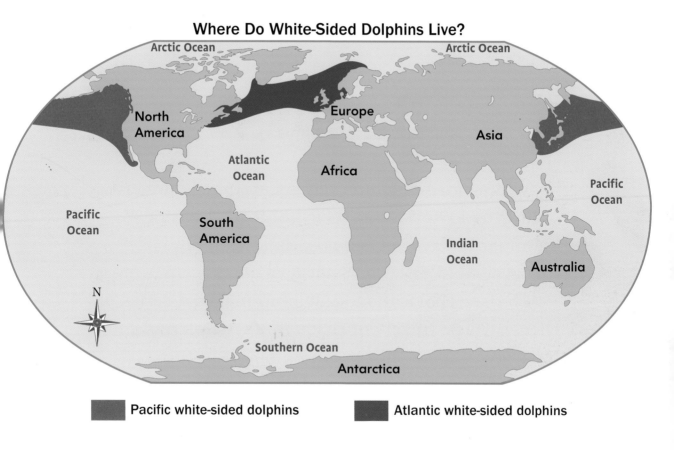

Pacific white-sided dolphins

Atlantic white-sided dolphins

white-sided dolphins like **continental shelves** and areas with deep underwater canyons.

Pacific white-sided dolphins **migrate** north in summer. In winter, some migrate inshore. Pacific white-sided dolphins enjoy continental shelf areas. They are also found farther offshore.

SENSES

    White-sided dolphins rely on an excellent sense of hearing to survive in their **habitat**. Hearing is an important part of echolocation. Dolphins use this system to discover what is around them.

    To use echolocation, a dolphin makes a series of clicks. These travel out through its **melon** and into the water. Then, they reach an object in the dolphin's path. They bounce off it and head back toward the dolphin.

    The dolphin listens for these echoes. They reveal the object's speed, distance, size, and shape. Echolocation gives the dolphin about as much information as sight gives a human.

    Dolphins also have keen eyesight. They can see well in and above water. Dolphins have a good sense of touch, too. Their smooth, rubbery skin is

very sensitive. Dolphins can also taste their food.
But, scientists do not think they have a sense of
smell.

Sound wave sent out by dolphin

Echo wave received by dolphin

DEFENSE

White-sided dolphins face danger from natural predators. For example, Pacific white-sided dolphins must watch out for killer whales.

White-sided dolphins can escape some dangers. They are fast swimmers. Their excellent sense of hearing also acts as a defense. They can listen for danger and communicate warnings to others.

Human activity also poses threats. Pollution affects dolphin **habitats**. In some areas, humans hunt white-sided dolphins. Other times, the dolphins become trapped accidentally in fishing nets. Human threats can be difficult to escape. But, fishing laws provide some protection.

A Pacific white-sided dolphin may become a meal for a killer whale.

FOOD

A white-sided dolphin's diet depends on its **habitat** and the season. Both species feed on squid. They also hunt various fish, including hakes and herring. The fish they eat provide the water they need. Dolphins don't drink salty seawater!

White-sided dolphins use echolocation to find their prey. Then, they feed as a group. A Pacific white-sided dolphin can dive for more than six minutes at a time to feed. An Atlantic white-sided dolphin can stay underwater for five minutes before surfacing to breathe.

Each dolphin grabs tasty treats with its sharp teeth. Pacific white-sided dolphins have up to 156 teeth. Up to 144 teeth fill an Atlantic white-sided

Pacific white-sided dolphins herd fish into a tight group to feed.

dolphin's mouth. These are for grasping, not
chewing. Dolphins swallow their prey in one big bite!

BABIES

Female white-sided dolphins reproduce every two to three years. After mating, a female Atlantic white-sided dolphin is **pregnant** for 11 months. A Pacific white-sided dolphin carries her young for 10 to 12 months. Dolphins almost always give birth to just one baby at a time. The baby is called a calf.

At birth, a white-sided calf measures up to 4 feet (1.2 m) long. An Atlantic white-sided calf weighs as much as 77 pounds (35 kg). A newborn Pacific white-sided calf is smaller. It only weighs around 33 pounds (15 kg).

Like other mammals, the mother dolphin makes milk for her calf. An Atlantic white-sided calf nurses for 18 months. A Pacific white-sided calf stops nursing after just 6 months.

The two white-sided dolphin species have different life spans. Atlantic white-sided dolphins live up to 27 years. Pacific white-sided dolphins can live more than 46 years!

To communicate, a white-sided calf will touch an adult with its flipper.

BEHAVIORS

Dolphins are social animals, and white-sided dolphins are no exception. Pacific white-sided dolphins form groups of 10 to 100 individuals. Sometimes, they form huge groups with more than 1,000 members!

Atlantic white-sided dolphin groups usually have 30 to 150 members. When **migrating** or feeding, those groups may join together. Then, a group has up to 500 members.

White-sided dolphins also swim around with other marine mammals. Pacific white-sided dolphins associate with fin whales, humpback whales, and white-beaked dolphins. The Atlantic species swims with northern right whale dolphins and Risso's dolphins.

White-sided dolphins are active at the water's surface. They often leap out of the water. Pacific white-sided dolphins will even turn somersaults! And, they **bow ride**. Both species are fascinating, important members of their cool **habitats**.

Pacific white-sided dolphins can leap 15 to 20 feet (5 to 6 m) out of the water!

WHITE-SIDED DOLPHIN FACTS

Scientific Name:

Atlantic white-sided dolphin *Lagenorhynchus acutus*

Pacific white-sided dolphin *Lagenorhynchus obliquidens*

Common Names:

Atlantic white-sided dolphin, lag

Pacific white-sided dolphin, lag

Average Size: Atlantic white-sided dolphins average 6 to 9 feet (1.9 to 2.8 m) in length. They weigh 365 to 510 pounds (165 to 230 kg). Pacific white-sided dolphins grow 6 to 8 feet (1.7 to 2.5 m) long. They weigh 190 to 400 pounds (85 to 180 kg).

Where They're Found: In the North Atlantic and North Pacific oceans

GLOSSARY

bow ride - to swim at the front of a boat or a whale. A dolphin uses the waves created there to assist movement and speed.

cetacean (sih-TAY-shuhn) - a member of the order Cetacea. Mammals such as dolphins, whales, and porpoises are cetaceans.

continental shelf - a shallow, underwater plain forming a continent's border. It ends with a steep slope to the deep ocean floor.

Delphinidae (dehl-FIHN-uh-dee) - the scientific name for the oceanic dolphin family. It includes dolphins that live mostly in salt water.

habitat - a place where a living thing is naturally found.

melon - a rounded structure found in the forehead of some cetaceans.

migrate - to move from one place to another, often to find food.

pregnant - having one or more babies growing within the body.

subpolar - relating to areas of cool water next to Earth's polar seas.

temperate - relating to an area where average temperatures range between 50 and 55 degrees Fahrenheit (10 and 13°C).

warm-blooded - having a body temperature that is not much affected by surrounding air or water.

WEB SITES

To learn more about white-sided dolphins, visit ABDO Publishing Company on the World Wide Web at **www.abdopublishing.com**. Web sites about white-sided dolphins are featured on our Book Links page. These links are routinely monitored and updated to provide the most current information available.

INDEX